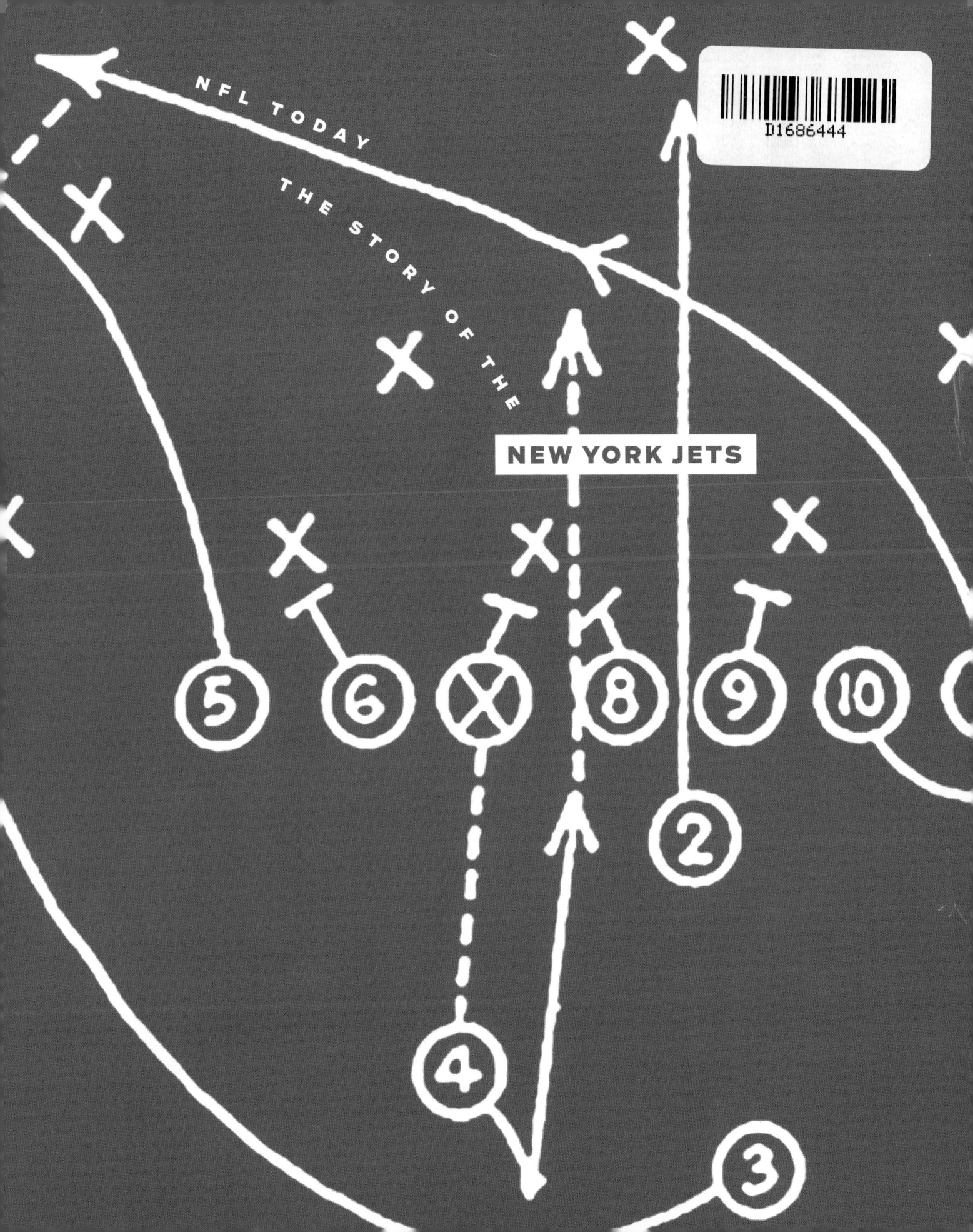

NFL TODAY
THE STORY OF THE
NEW YORK JETS

NFL TODAY

THE STORY OF THE NEW YORK JETS

JIM WHITING

PUBLISHED BY CREATIVE PAPERBACKS
P.O. BOX 227, MANKATO, MINNESOTA 56002
CREATIVE PAPERBACKS IS AN IMPRINT OF THE CREATIVE COMPANY
WWW.THECREATIVECOMPANY.US

DESIGN AND PRODUCTION BY BLUE DESIGN
ART DIRECTION BY RITA MARSHALL
PRINTED IN THE UNITED STATES OF AMERICA

PHOTOGRAPHS BY CORBIS (DAVID BERGMAN, LOUIE PSIHOYOS/SCIENCE FACTION) GETTY IMAGES (BRIAN BAHR, AL BELLO, DAVID BERGMAN/SPORTS ILLUSTRATED, TIM CLARY/AFP, JAMES DRAKE/SPORTS ILLUSTRATED, DAVID DRAPKIN, FOCUS ON SPORT, HARRY HOW, MARK KAUFFMAN/TIME & LIFE PICTURES, NICK LAHAM, LONNIE MAJOR/ALLSPORT, JIM MCISAAC, VIC MILTON/NFL, RONALD C. MODRA/SPORTS IMAGERY, NFL, DARRYL NORENBERG/NFL, BERNIE NUNEZ, AL PEREIRA, AL PEREIRA/NEW YORK JETS, RICH SCHULTZ, COREY SIPKIN/NY DAILY NEWS ARCHIVE, RICK STEWART, KEVIN TERRELL, ROB TRINGALI/SPORTSCHROME, JIM TURNER/NFL, CHARLES AQUA VIVA, LOU WITT/NFL)

COPYRIGHT © 2014 CREATIVE PAPERBACKS

INTERNATIONAL COPYRIGHT RESERVED IN ALL COUNTRIES. NO PART OF THIS BOOK MAY BE REPRODUCED IN ANY FORM WITHOUT WRITTEN PERMISSION FROM THE PUBLISHER.

LIBRARY OF CONGRESS CATALOGING-IN-PUBLICATION DATA
WHITING, JIM.
THE STORY OF THE NEW YORK JETS / BY JIM WHITING.
P. CM. — (NFL TODAY)
INCLUDES INDEX.
SUMMARY: THE HISTORY OF THE NATIONAL FOOTBALL LEAGUE'S NEW YORK JETS, SURVEYING THE FRANCHISE'S BIGGEST STARS AND MOST MEMORABLE MOMENTS FROM ITS INAUGURAL SEASON IN 1960 TO TODAY.
ISBN 978-1-60818-313-5 (HARDCOVER)
ISBN 978-0-89812-866-6 (PBK)
1. NEW YORK JETS (FOOTBALL TEAM)—HISTORY—JUVENILE LITERATURE. I. TITLE.

GV956.N37W45 2013
796.332'64097471—DC23   2012033812

FIRST EDITION
9 8 7 6 5 4 3 2 1

COVER: TACKLE D'BRICKASHAW FERGUSON
PAGE 2: DEFENSIVE TACKLE SIONE POUHA
PAGES 4–5: QUARTERBACK JOE NAMATH
PAGE 6: WIDE RECEIVER JUSTIN MCCAREINS

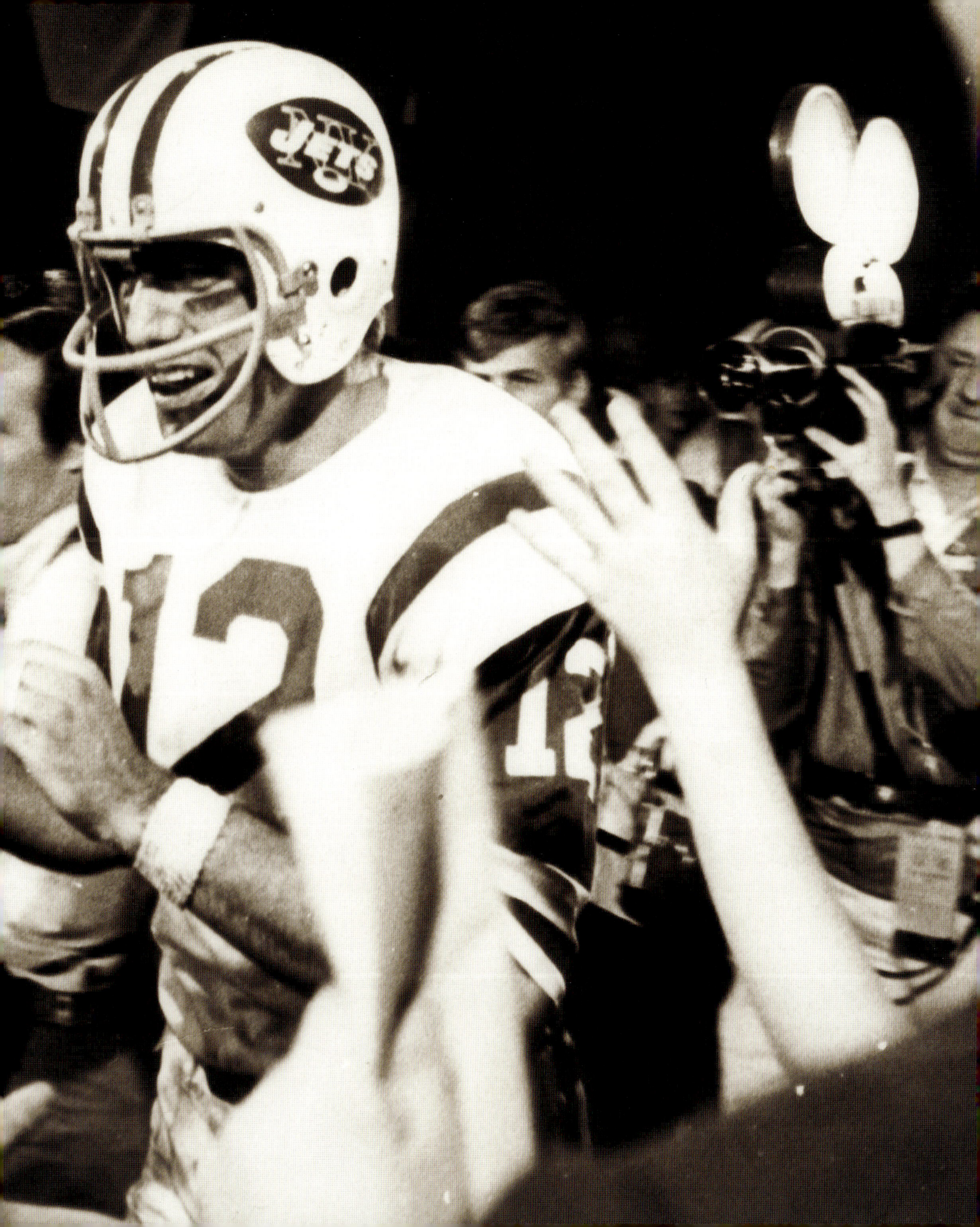
JETS
12

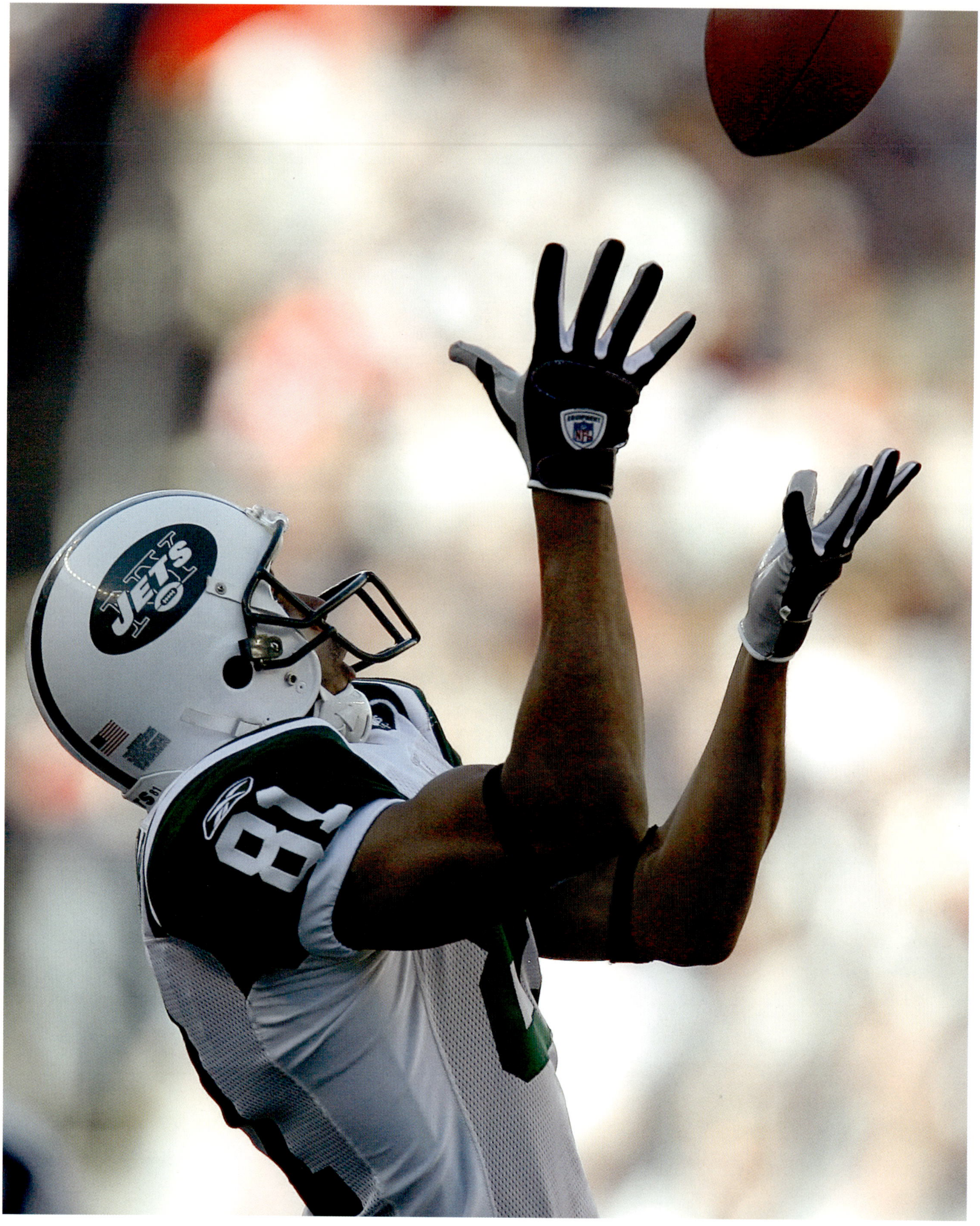
JETS
81

TABLE OF CONTENTS

BIRTH OF THE TITANS 8

JOE'S PROMISE 18

A BIG APPLE REBUILD 26

THE BIG BAD JETS 34

SIDELINE STORIES

TITAN-IC TROUBLES 13

THE HEIDI GAME 17

NAMATH'S BOOTLEG 22

LEARNING TO WALK AGAIN 25

THE MONDAY NIGHT MIRACLE 32

FIREMAN ED 41

MEET THE JETS

DON MAYNARD 10

JOE NAMATH 16

JOE KLECKO 20

WAYNE CHREBET 28

CURTIS MARTIN 38

REX RYAN 43

INDEX 48

TIMES SQUARE IS A BUSY AND LIGHT-FILLED INTERSECTION IN NEW YORK CITY

Birth of the Titans

New York is famous for many things—perhaps most of all the towering skyscrapers that made it one of the world's first vertical cities. So it's ironic that its most famous nickname, "The Big Apple," originated in a humble horse stable hundreds of miles away. Sports reporter John Fitz Gerald is generally credited with coining the name in the early 1920s. Fitz Gerald especially liked horse racing, and he wrote, "The Big Apple. The dream of every lad that ever threw a leg over a thoroughbred and the goal of all horsemen. There's only one Big Apple. That's New York." The term came to him when he overheard two men walking their horses around a stable in New Orleans. One asked the other where he was heading next. "The Big Apple," was the proud reply.

A similar pride animated former broadcaster Harry Wismer in 1960 as he and the other founders of the fledgling American Football League (AFL) mounted a challenge to the older, well-established National Football League (NFL). The AFL put a team in New

FULLBACK BILL MATHIS WAS AN ALL-PRO FOR THE TITANS IN 1961

MEET THE JETS

Don Maynard

WIDE RECEIVER / TITANS/JETS SEASONS: 1960–72 / HEIGHT: 6 FEET / WEIGHT: 180 POUNDS

When coach Sammy Baugh was putting together the first roster for the New York Titans in 1960, he remembered fellow Texan Don Maynard, a fleet-footed receiver then playing football in Canada. Baugh convinced team owner Harry Wismer to sign Maynard to the team's first contract. For the next 13 years, Maynard would play a vital role in the New York offense. During 5 of those seasons, he caught 50 or more passes for more than 1,000 yards each year. Maynard was renowned for his ability to improvise on the field. He would find a way to get open, even in the tightest coverage. Then he would use his outstanding speed to catch up with tosses from the team's quarterback. Once quarterback Joe Namath joined the Jets in 1965, the Namath-to-Maynard combination became one of the most lethal in the AFL. The pair clicked for two touchdowns in the AFL Championship Game in 1968, including the game winner. When Maynard retired in 1973, he held pro football records for career catches (633) and receiving yards (11,834).

DON MAYNARD (#13) WAS A RELIABLE TARGET FOR JETS QUARTERBACKS

York, and Wismer became the owner of the New York Titans. Wismer immediately challenged the Giants, the city's NFL team, by proclaiming, "We're called Titans because titans are bigger than giants."

The Titans posted a respectable 7–7 record their first year, with a potent offense that revolved around quarterback Al Dorow and receivers Art Powell and Don Maynard. Maynard became the team's first star. With his outstanding speed and elusive moves, he scored 88 touchdowns during his career (still a club record) and eventually earned a place in the Pro Football Hall of Fame.

Unfortunately, the Titans struggled at the ticket office. Part of the problem was their home venue, the aging Polo Grounds (where baseball's New York Giants had played before moving to San Francisco in 1958). Average home attendance the first season was about 15,000, and 2 years later it dwindled to just over 5,000. Wismer couldn't pay players' salaries, and a group led by former television executive David "Sonny" Werblin purchased the franchise.

"He comes to play, and he comes to win."

DON MAYNARD ON JOE NAMATH

Werblin gave the club a complete makeover, changing its name to the peppier-sounding Jets and replacing the players' drab blue-and-gold uniforms with brighter kelly green and white. He also brought in veteran coach Weeb Ewbank. Ewbank, who had led the Baltimore Colts to two NFL championships, didn't try to fire up players by yelling at them. "Weeb Ewbank treated us like men, and I appreciated that," recalled center John Schmitt.

Despite their losing record (5–8–1) in 1963, Ewbank's Jets began building fan support. The fans had even more to cheer about the next season when the team moved to Shea Stadium in the New York City borough of Queens and featured a new star, 1964 AFL Rookie of the Year running back Matt Snell.

The excitement reached a fever pitch in 1965 when flashy quarterback Joe Namath arrived from the University of Alabama. Werblin convinced Namath to join the AFL instead of the NFL by offering him a 3-year contract for the then amazing sum of $427,000, making him the highest-paid American athlete in any sport. With his good looks and cocky attitude, "Broadway Joe" became a star both on the field and off.

Namath's teammates weren't jealous of the attention Broadway Joe commanded. Instead, they were impressed by the quarterback's work ethic. "He paid the price," said Maynard. "He worked just as hard and studied just as much film as anybody else. In that way, naturally, you accept the guy for what he does. He comes to play, and he comes to win."

SIDELINE STORIES

Titan-ic Troubles

When the AFL was established in 1960, most of its franchises' owners were wealthy businessmen. That was not true of Titans owner Harry Wismer, a fast-talking sports broadcaster known for occasionally stretching the truth. During his three years as owner, the team was a financial bust. The club scrounged for practice fields and played home games before tiny crowds in the decaying Polo Grounds. To reduce expenses, Wismer stopped paying many bills, including hotel tabs and salary checks. Frustrated players finally took a stand in 1962, refusing to board the plane for an away game in Denver unless their salaries were guaranteed. That was one reason why offensive tackle Alex Kroll wrote, "The Titans of '62 stand unchallenged as the worst-managed, most-unprofessional professional team of the modern era." Eventually, the league took over the Titans to ensure that the AFL kept a team in New York. Despite his financial woes and questionable behavior, Wismer had several positive effects. He used his newspaper contacts to boost coverage for the league. Much more importantly, he originated the concept of revenue sharing, in which all eight teams received an equal amount of money from the league's television contract.

AL DOROW WAS THE FIRST QUARTERBACK FOR THE NEW YORK TITANS

THE JETS FOUND STAR POWER WITH BROADWAY JOE AND COACH EWBANK

Namath proved he was worth every penny. In 1966, he led the Jets to a 6–6–2 record by throwing long bombs to Maynard and second-year receiver George Sauer Jr. Everything was looking bright for the Jets until Namath began struggling with knee problems.

Namath played through the pain the next year, leading the Jets to their first winning record (8–5–1) and becoming the first quarterback in either the AFL or NFL to pass for more than 4,000 yards in a season. Rookie running back Emerson Boozer, meanwhile, paired with Snell to give New York perhaps the AFL's best rushing duo. The Jets were ready to soar.

MEET THE JETS

Joe Namath

QUARTERBACK / JETS SEASONS: 1965–76 / HEIGHT: 6-FOOT-2 / WEIGHT: 200 POUNDS

Legendary University of Alabama coach Paul "Bear" Bryant called Joe Namath "the greatest athlete I've ever coached," and later Jets owner Woody Johnson called him "the most important player in the history of this franchise." Namath was not only a football star, he was also a league maker. Namath's decision to sign with the Jets instead of the NFL's St. Louis (now Arizona) Cardinals in 1965 brought the AFL credibility it had not previously achieved with sportswriters or fans. Soon, New York fans packed Shea Stadium for Jets games, the local press expanded its coverage of the AFL, and television ratings for AFL contests soared. When Namath upheld his guarantee of victory in Super Bowl III, NFL owners began to see the economic value of merging the two leagues. On the field, Namath had a lightning-quick delivery and a cannon arm. "He could throw a ball through a wall," said Jets center John Schmitt. Off the field, he was treated as a celebrity of the highest order and was once paid $10,000 to shave off his mustache for a shaving cream commercial.

SIDELINE STORIES

The Heidi Game

The Jets' 1968 season featured not only an unexpected Super Bowl victory but also two remarkable games against the Oakland Raiders. The Jets won the more important contest—a come-from-behind victory in the AFL Championship Game. However, an earlier game that they lost became even more famous. The game took place in Oakland but drew a large television audience in New York. The lead seesawed back and forth until, with 65 seconds to go (and at nearly 7:00 P.M. in the East), New York's Jim Turner kicked what seemed to be the winning field goal. At least that's what Jets fans thought; they never got to see the game's final minute. Because the television network broadcasting the game had previously committed to show the family film *Heidi* at 7:00 P.M., it cut away from the game on the East Coast. New Yorkers never saw Oakland stun the Jets with two lightning-quick touchdowns to win 43–32. Outraged fans bombarded their local stations with calls. In a nationwide poll taken years later, football fans voted "The Heidi Game" as one of the all-time most memorable games.

FULLBACK MATT SNELL CARRIED THE BALL IN THE INFAMOUS "HEIDI GAME"

Joe's Promise

Jets fans had high expectations in 1968. The club had the league's top quarterback directing one of the AFL's best offenses, as well as a great defense led by end Gerry Philbin, linebacker Al Atkinson, and cornerback Johnny Sample. The Jets finished with an 11–3 record to top the Eastern Division of the AFL and advanced to the AFL Championship Game against the Oakland Raiders.

In a tight battle at Shea Stadium, New York edged Oakland 27–23, thanks to three Namath touchdown passes and two field goals by kicker Jim Turner. Namath didn't remember much of that game after suffering a concussion in the second quarter. Still, he led a late fourth-quarter drive for the winning touchdown.

The next stop on the "Jets Express" was Miami, where New York faced the NFL champion Baltimore Colts in Super Bowl III. Only die-hard New York or AFL

EMERSON BOOZER GAVE FUEL TO THE JETS EXPRESS'S SUPER BOWL RUN

MEET THE JETS

Joe Klecko

DEFENSIVE TACKLE/END / JETS SEASONS: 1977–87 / HEIGHT: 6-FOOT-3 / WEIGHT: 263 POUNDS

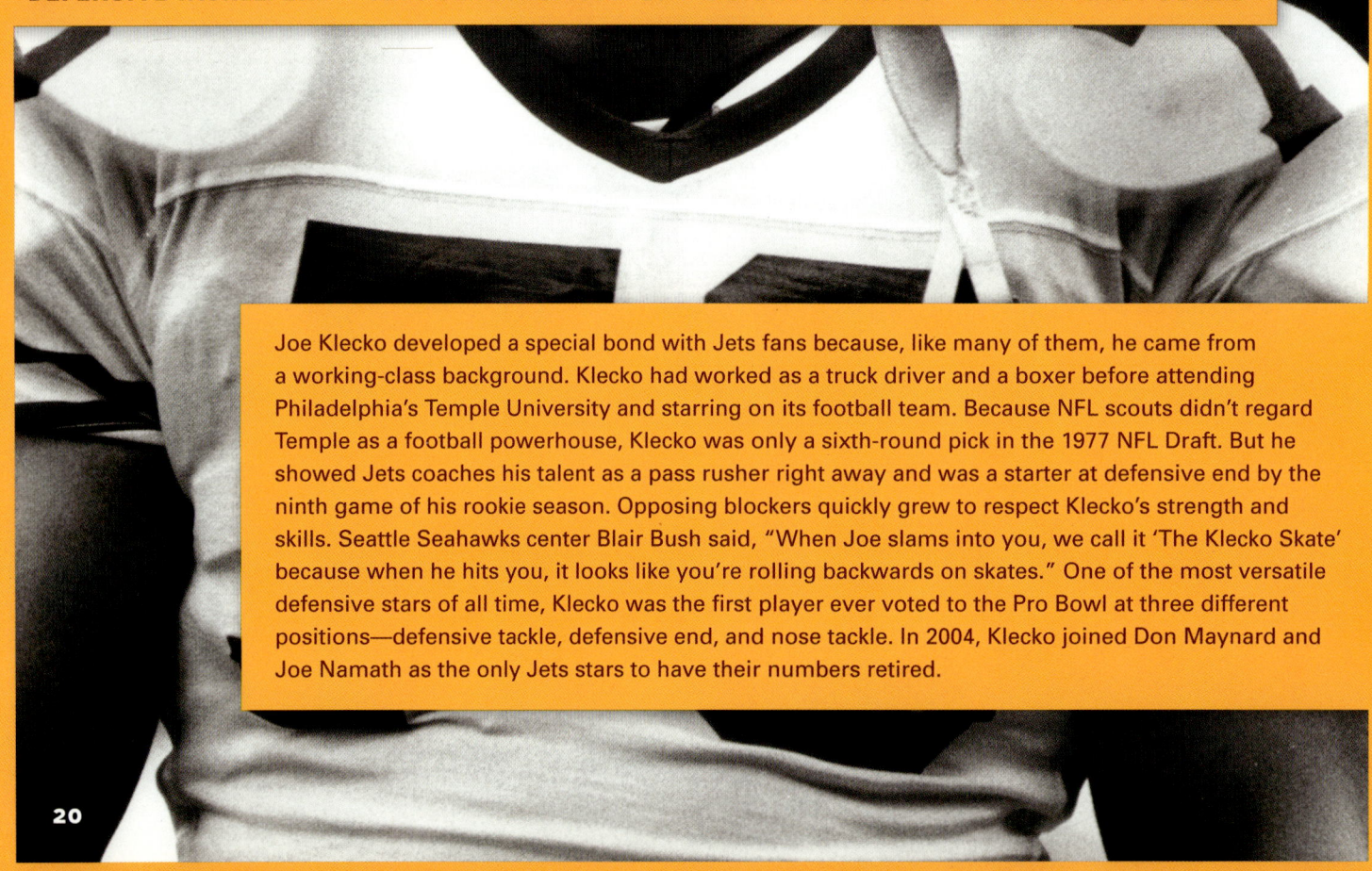

Joe Klecko developed a special bond with Jets fans because, like many of them, he came from a working-class background. Klecko had worked as a truck driver and a boxer before attending Philadelphia's Temple University and starring on its football team. Because NFL scouts didn't regard Temple as a football powerhouse, Klecko was only a sixth-round pick in the 1977 NFL Draft. But he showed Jets coaches his talent as a pass rusher right away and was a starter at defensive end by the ninth game of his rookie season. Opposing blockers quickly grew to respect Klecko's strength and skills. Seattle Seahawks center Blair Bush said, "When Joe slams into you, we call it 'The Klecko Skate' because when he hits you, it looks like you're rolling backwards on skates." One of the most versatile defensive stars of all time, Klecko was the first player ever voted to the Pro Bowl at three different positions—defensive tackle, defensive end, and nose tackle. In 2004, Klecko joined Don Maynard and Joe Namath as the only Jets stars to have their numbers retired.

"In fact, I guarantee it."

JOE NAMATH PROMISES A SUPER BOWL VICTORY AGAINST THE COLTS

fans believed the Jets had any chance. The Colts featured such future Hall-of-Famers as quarterback Johnny Unitas and tight end John Mackey. Some writers predicted the Colts would win by as much as 30 points. Namath had other ideas. "We're going to win Sunday," he boldly announced. "In fact, I guarantee it."

Coach Ewbank was furious after learning of the guarantee. "You can't go talking like this and giving the Colts fuel," he said. But Namath's words charged up his own teammates more than the Colts. Millions of fans watched in disbelief as the Jets scored first on a Snell touchdown, and their defense refused to budge throughout the game. The 16–7 Jets win was one of the most shocking upsets in sports history. It was also a turning point in professional football, proving that AFL teams were competitive and helping to pave the way for a merger of the two leagues before the 1970 season.

Jets fans were confident that Namath's arm could carry them to more titles. Unfortunately, his battered knees and injuries to other team leaders grounded the Jets. After joining the NFL in 1970, the Jets settled near the middle of the American Football Conference (AFC) standings. Namath remained a fine passer, and receiver Jerome Barkum and flamboyant running back John Riggins added power to the offense. But the club's record continued to slide.

When the Jets won a total of only six games in 1975 and 1976, the team's owners started making changes. First, a new coach—former Cleveland Browns linebacker Walt Michaels—was brought in.

SIDELINE STORIES

Namath's Bootleg

Joe Namath's guarantee before Super Bowl III was not his only daring prediction during his Jets career. He made another bold one midway through the 1974 season. The Jets were 1–7, and Namath's ailing knees were causing him to have a miserable year. Still, "Broadway Joe" predicted that the team would win its final six games and finish with a .500 record. Amazingly, that is just what the Jets did, beginning with an overtime victory against the New York Giants. That game featured one of the most unforgettable plays in team history. Trailing 20–13 late in the fourth quarter, the Jets had the ball on the Giants' three-yard line. Namath called a running play for halfback Emerson Boozer, but at the last second he surprised everyone by faking to Boozer and taking the ball himself in a stiff-legged bootleg to the left. Just as he limped across the goal line, two Giants players closed in, but Namath raised his arm as if to say, "Don't touch me," and the defenders held back. A few minutes later, the Jets won the game in overtime to start their six-game winning streak.

OPPOSING QUARTERBACKS FEARED JETS SACK-MASTER MARK GASTINEAU (LEFT)

Michaels turned the offense over to young quarterback Richard Todd and released Namath. Broadway Joe ended his New York career with more than 27,000 passing yards and 170 touchdowns—club records that still stand today.

Michaels's Jets, featuring Todd and defensive ends Joe Klecko and Mark Gastineau, began revving up Shea Stadium crowds in the late 1970s. Klecko and Gastineau joined with defensive tackles Marty Lyons and Abdul Salaam to form a hard-rushing defensive line nicknamed "The New York Sack Exchange." Gastineau earned both cheers and jeers when he celebrated his sacks by dancing over the fallen quarterback. Outraged owners of other NFL teams soon passed the "Gastineau Rule" to outlaw such showy celebrations.

In 1981, the Jets reached the NFL playoffs for the first time. In the opening round, the Jets fell behind the Buffalo Bills 24–0, made a remarkable comeback, but finally lost 31–27. Coach Michaels wasn't discouraged. "If all of New York hasn't fallen in love with this team yet," he said, "then they will in 1982."

PAT LEAHY SPENT HIS ENTIRE 18-YEAR CAREER KICKING FOR THE JETS

The 1982 Jets advanced all the way to the AFC Championship Game before losing 14–0 to the Dolphins on a muddy field in Miami's Orange Bowl. Michaels retired after the loss and was replaced by Joe Walton. Before the 1984 season, the club moved its home base across the Hudson River to Giants Stadium (which Jets players and fans preferred to call "the Meadowlands"). Fans filled the larger stadium with even louder shouts of "J–E–T–S! Jets! Jets! Jets!"

The loudest cheers were reserved for quarterback Ken O'Brien, halfback Freeman McNeil, and wide receiver Al Toon, who led the club back to the playoffs in 1985. Fans became even more excited in 1986, when the Jets got off to a 10–1 start. Then O'Brien, Klecko, and several other key players went down with injuries, and the Jets lost their final five games, limping into the playoffs. They made a great showing in the postseason, however, first defeating the Kansas City Chiefs and then taking the Cleveland Browns into double-overtime before losing 23–20.

The Jets then seemed to lose their winning altitude and slipped down the AFC standings for the rest of the decade. Even the outstanding efforts of Pro-Bowlers such as safety Erik McMillan and tight end Mickey Shuler couldn't halt the slide. After a miserable 4–12 season in 1989, Walton was fired.

SIDELINE STORIES

Learning to Walk Again

At 6-foot-5 and 275 pounds, defensive end Dennis Byrd (pictured) was big and powerful. He seemed destined for NFL stardom until November 29, 1992, when his career came to a crashing halt. Playing against the Kansas City Chiefs at the Meadowlands, Byrd and fellow defensive end Scott Mersereau rushed Chiefs quarterback Dave Krieg from opposite sides. When Krieg slid forward, the two defenders collided, and Byrd slammed his helmet into Mersereau's chest. While fans stood stunned, Jets trainers stabilized Byrd's broken neck before putting him on a stretcher, probably saving his life. For the next week, Byrd lay in a hospital, totally paralyzed. Then doctors noticed a slight movement in his big toe. The good news was relayed to Jets players before the start of their next game against the Buffalo Bills. They responded with a 24–17 upset win and later delivered the game ball to Byrd's hospital room. Through months of hard work, Byrd learned to walk again. Following his recovery, Byrd established a camp near his home in Oklahoma to help improve the lives of physically challenged children.

VINNY TESTAVERDE AND BILL PARCELLS TOOK THE JETS BACK TO THE PLAYOFFS

A Big Apple Rebuild

The Jets made it back to the playoffs in 1991 but took another nosedive in the two seasons that followed. After yet another losing campaign in 1994, team owner Leon Hess announced, "I'm 80 years old, and I want results now. I'm entitled to some enjoyment from this team, and that means winning."

Hess then made a disastrous decision, turning the club over to former NFL tight end Rich Kotite, who had recently been fired as coach of the Philadelphia Eagles. The easygoing Kotite had trouble enforcing his rules on players, and the Jets plummeted to a 3–13 record in 1995. "This is about as bad as you're ever going to see," Kotite remarked at the end of the season, but he was wrong. The next year, the club managed to win only one game. Kotite was then replaced by a man who knew a lot about winning in Giants Stadium, former New York Giants coach Bill Parcells.

Parcells was a legendary football figure in New York, having coached the Giants from 1983 to 1990 and led them to Super Bowl victories in 1986 and 1990. After a

OUTSPOKEN RECEIVER KEYSHAWN JOHNSON BEGAN HIS CAREER WITH NEW YORK

MEET THE JETS

Wayne Chrebet
WIDE RECEIVER / JETS SEASONS: 1995–2005 / HEIGHT: 5-FOOT-10 / WEIGHT: 188 POUNDS

Wayne Chrebet had everything going against him when he asked the Jets for a tryout during the summer of 1995. He was smaller than most professional wide receivers, had played at tiny Hofstra University on New York's Long Island, and had not been drafted by any pro team. In fact, when Chrebet showed up for his first Jets workout, the team's security guard didn't want to let him in. But what Chrebet had going for him was his incredible courage: he was not afraid to run pass routes across the middle of the field, where huge linebackers and safeties might crush him to try to dislodge the ball from his hands. Amazingly, Chrebet not only made the team in 1995 but became one of its offensive stars for 11 seasons. By the time he was forced to retire after suffering a series of concussions, Chrebet ranked second in the Jets' record book in receptions, third in receiving yards, and third in touchdown passes caught. A favorite in New York, scores of fans showed up to games wearing his number 80 jersey.

JONATHAN GOODWIN AND KEVIN MAWAE SOLIDIFIED THE JETS' OFFENSIVE LINE

three-year attempt at retirement, he had then returned to the game and transformed a broken-down New England Patriots team into a Super Bowl contender. Hess now offered Parcells a new challenge back in New York.

Parcells's lineup featured two key offensive weapons: receivers Wayne Chrebet and Keyshawn Johnson. The two were as different as night and day. The 5-foot-10 Chrebet was quiet, steady, and tough—more of a hard worker than a natural athlete. At 6-foot-4, Johnson was tall and smooth. He was also talkative and flashy.

Under Parcells's magic touch, the Jets jumped to a 9–7 record in 1997. The coach promised his players that even better times lay ahead. "I told them that nobody could stand still," he recalled. "You either get better, or you get worse. It's that simple."

To improve the team's chances, Parcells signed three free agents—running back Curtis Martin, center Kevin Mawae, and quarterback Vinny Testaverde. The new arrivals helped turn the Jets into an offensive powerhouse in 1998 and led the club to its first division title since its AFL days.

In the playoffs, the Jets defeated the Jacksonville Jaguars 34–24 to reach the AFC Championship Game opposite the Denver Broncos, the defending Super Bowl champions. In the title contest, Denver capitalized on six New York turnovers to crush the Jets' Super Bowl dreams 23–10.

Parcells stepped down after the 1999 season and handed the coaching reins to former assistant Al Groh. Groh led the Jets for only one year before resigning to become a college coach, but he made a key move that would brighten the club's future—selecting quarterback Chad Pennington in the first round of the 2000 NFL Draft.

The Jets were impressed with Pennington's accurate throwing arm, his commanding size (6-foot-3 and 225 pounds), and his intelligence. Pennington sat on the Jets' bench for two years until new coach Herm Edwards put him in the lineup midway through the 2002 season. Under Pennington, the Jets rebounded from a 2–5 start to finish the year as AFC East Division champs with a 9–7 record, putting them in the postseason again. Pennington's poise

CHAD PENNINGTON PASSED THE JETS INTO THE PLAYOFFS IN 2004 AND 2006

SIDELINE STORIES

The Monday Night Miracle

As the third quarter of the Jets' *Monday Night Football* game on October 23, 2000, ended with the Miami Dolphins leading 30–7, the team's broadcaster, Howard Davis, said, "This game is over." After all, the Dolphins had allowed just 51 points in the season's first six games. Then Jets quarterback Vinny Testaverde, who had thrown three interceptions earlier in the game, went to work. Touchdown pass. Touchdown pass. Field goal. Touchdown pass. In just over 11 minutes, the score was tied 30–30. Although Miami scored on a long pass two plays later, the Jets wouldn't give up. With less than a minute to go, they were on the Dolphins' three-yard line. Coach Al Groh called a tackle-eligible pass to 300-pound tackle Jumbo Elliott, who awkwardly bobbled the ball but held on for the catch to tie the score. In overtime, an interception by Jets safety Marcus Coleman set up a game-winning field goal that completed the second-greatest comeback in NFL history. Two years later, fans in a national poll voted the "Monday Night Miracle" as the greatest *Monday Night Football* game to that point.

JUMBO ELLIOTT BECAME THE UNLIKELY HERO OF THE "MONDAY NIGHT MIRACLE"

DOUG BRIEN MADE SOME CLUTCH KICKS IN THE 2004 POSTSEASON

impressed fans, coaches, and teammates. "Chad is like a coach on the field," said Jets tight end Anthony Becht. "He understands everything. He knows what has to be done in every situation."

Optimism was high in the Meadowlands before the 2003 season. But in a preseason game against the Giants, Pennington was slammed to the ground, shattering his wrist. By the time he returned two months later, the Jets were in last place in the AFC East and doomed to suffer another losing season.

In 2004, Pennington, now fully recovered, directed the Jets to a 5–0 start by utilizing a "West Coast" offense that featured short passes to receivers Justin McCareins and Santana Moss, and slashing runs by Martin. The Jets finished 10–6 and qualified for the playoffs.

The Jets' postseason adventure that year featured two 20–17 overtime contests. New York won the first, defeating the San Diego Chargers on a Doug Brien field goal in the extra session. The following week, the team traveled to Pittsburgh to take on the powerful Steelers and nearly won that game as well. But the Steelers rallied to tie the contest 17–17 late in the fourth quarter and won it on an overtime field goal. Reporters asked Coach Edwards if he was satisfied with how his club had rebounded from its last-place finish the previous year. "We're excited, but we're not satisfied," he said. "No, no, we won't be satisfied until we win the championship."

33

ERIC MANGINI EARNED THE NICKNAME "MANGENIUS" HIS FIRST SEASON

The Big Bad Jets

The club's championship dreams quickly faded the next year, though, when Pennington suffered a shoulder injury in the third game of the season. Then Martin went down with a knee injury that effectively ended not only the Jets' postseason hopes but also the career of one of the NFL's all-time leading rushers.

Jets management then decided to go in an entirely new direction, replacing Edwards with 35-year-old Eric Mangini, who had spent the previous few seasons as defensive coordinator for the New England Patriots. Now he was taking the reins of the Patriots' biggest rival. "I know how passionate the Jets fans are," Mangini said. "I've been here with them and I've played against them, and I'm a lot happier to be here with them."

No one expected the Jets to go far under their youthful rookie coach in 2006, but Mangini brought a new fire to the Meadowlands, inspiring the team to a solid 10–6 record. Some writers referred to the new winning spirit in New York as "Mangini Magic." The most magical game of the season took place on a rainy Sunday in

THE JETS STUCK TOGETHER THROUGH A TOUGH, FOUR-WIN 2007

36

RECEIVER LAVERANUES COLES WAS A DEEP THREAT WITH HIS TRACK-STAR SPEED

MEET THE JETS

Curtis Martin

RUNNING BACK / JETS SEASONS: 1998–2005 / HEIGHT: 5-FOOT-11 / WEIGHT: 210 POUNDS

Growing up in Pittsburgh, Pennsylvania, Curtis Martin never dreamed of playing professional football. In fact, he didn't even join his high school team until his senior year, when his mother insisted he take part in a school activity to keep him out of trouble. Martin quickly proved that he had the talent to succeed as a college running back at the University of Pittsburgh and then as a pro with the New England Patriots under coach Bill Parcells. In 1998, one year after Parcells moved on to the Jets, he brought Martin to New York. Signing Martin cost the Jets two high draft picks, but Parcells said, "He's worth twice the price." Martin topped the 1,000-yard mark each of the next 7 seasons with the Jets and led the NFL in rushing in 2004. Despite his success, Martin was always humble and even-tempered. Jets offensive coordinator Paul Hackett called him "the quiet superstar." He was also a very generous man, donating more than 10 percent of his earnings to a foundation he formed to help people who were homeless or jobless.

SANTANA MOSS PLAYED HIS LAST SEASON WITH THE JETS IN 2004

November, when Mangini's Jets stunned his former team, the powerful Patriots, 17–14. The two teams met again during the playoffs, with New England winning, 37–16. Despite the loss, Mangini and the Jets players felt that they had made an important statement—the club was definitely on the upward trend again.

Even after a subpar 2007 when the Jets won just four games, mostly because of injuries to key players, optimism remained high in the Meadowlands. That optimism grew just before the start of the 2008 season when the Jets obtained future Hall-of-Famer Brett Favre in a trade with the Green Bay Packers. The 38-year-old quarterback proved that he still had his winning touch as he slung the ball to receivers Laveranues Coles and Jerricho Cotchery. Thanks to their efforts and those of such players as running back

39

IN 2008, NFL ALL-TIME PASSING LEADER BRETT FAVRE CAME TO THE JETS

Thomas Jones and cornerback Darrelle Revis, the Jets won five straight games at midseason to go to 8–3. Unfortunately, Favre and his teammates fell out of sync, and New York dropped four of its last five games—a disappointing losing skid that knocked the Jets from playoff contention and prompted team owners to fire Mangini. His replacement was former Baltimore Ravens defensive coordinator Rex Ryan.

Four months later, the Jets cut a deal with Mangini, now the new coach of the Cleveland Browns, to trade up 12 spots in the 2009 NFL Draft and nab University of Southern California quarterback Mark Sanchez as their quarterback of the future. "We saw the great feet, the poise, and how confident he was," Ryan said after the team ran him through a private pre-draft workout. "We knew, I think, right then that this was the guy we really wanted."

When the 2009 Jets fell to 7–7 in late December, Ryan publicly said his team was out of the playoffs. Almost certainly they would have been, facing undefeated Indianapolis on the road in the season's next-to-last game. But Colts coach Jim Caldwell made the controversial decision to rest his starters for much of the second half in preparation for the playoffs rather than try to match the 1972 Miami Dolphins as the only NFL team ever to have a perfect record. Down 15–10 at that point, the Jets came back to win 29–15. The following week, the Jets punched their postseason ticket by crushing the playoff-bound Cincinnati Bengals, who kept most of their starters glued to the bench for the entire game.

New York faced Cincinnati again in the first round and emerged with a 24–14 victory. Incredibly, a win

SIDELINE STORIES

Fireman Ed

Every NFL team has its special fans, and many have cheerleaders. But the Jets had both in one person—"Fireman Ed" Anzalone. Beginning when the Jets moved to the Meadowlands in 1984, Anzalone led the crowds in chanting, "J-E-T-S, Jets! Jets! Jets!" numerous times each game. He did his cheerleading perched on the shoulders of another "superfan" while usually wearing a number 42 Jets jersey (in honor of former running back Bruce Harper) and a green fireman's helmet similar to the one he wore on the job as a New York City firefighter. The first time he led the chant, Anzalone tried standing on the front-row railing so he could be seen. But when he nearly toppled over, his brother put him on his shoulders. Within a few games, Fireman Ed had at least 5,000 fans chanting along with him. Soon, the entire stadium began rocking with the cheer. "I feel I make a difference," Anzalone once told reporters. "Seventy-six thousand fans give me the opportunity each week to get something done, to make a home-field advantage for our team." In 2012, he announced that he would remain a Jets fan but no longer play his superfan role.

SHONN GREENE SCORED 18 TOUCHDOWNS IN HIS FIRST 4 SEASONS

the following week put the Jets into the AFC Championship Game against Indianapolis. The shocking run ended there, though. After taking an early 17–6 lead, the Jets collapsed as the Colts roared back for a 30–17 triumph.

Before the 2010 season, Ryan made headlines by predicting that his team would win the Super Bowl. "I believe we'll do it," he explained, "so why wouldn't we say it?" Ryan nearly proved to be a prophet. After an 11–5 regular season, the Jets again won their first two playoff games. But they fell behind Pittsburgh 24–0 in the AFC title game. A late rally was squashed as the Jets just missed the Super Bowl for the second year in a row, 24–19.

With two Super Bowl near misses, New York fans looked forward to the 2011 season. "Rex Ryan has instilled a sense of swagger and bravado that has played very well in New York…," noted one Big Apple sportswriter. "There is a lot to like here." But the Jets proved to be inconsistent, assembling two three-game winning streaks but also two three-game losing skids. The resulting 8–8 mark left them outside the playoffs.

Still, the Jets faithful remained hopeful. With Sanchez, running back Shonn Greene, and guard Matt Slauson, New York had a formidable offense to go along with a stout defense led by Revis. The excitement rose another notch in the off-season when the Jets added former Denver quarterback Tim Tebow to the roster as Sanchez's backup. Tebow had led the Broncos to several miraculous comeback

MEET THE JETS

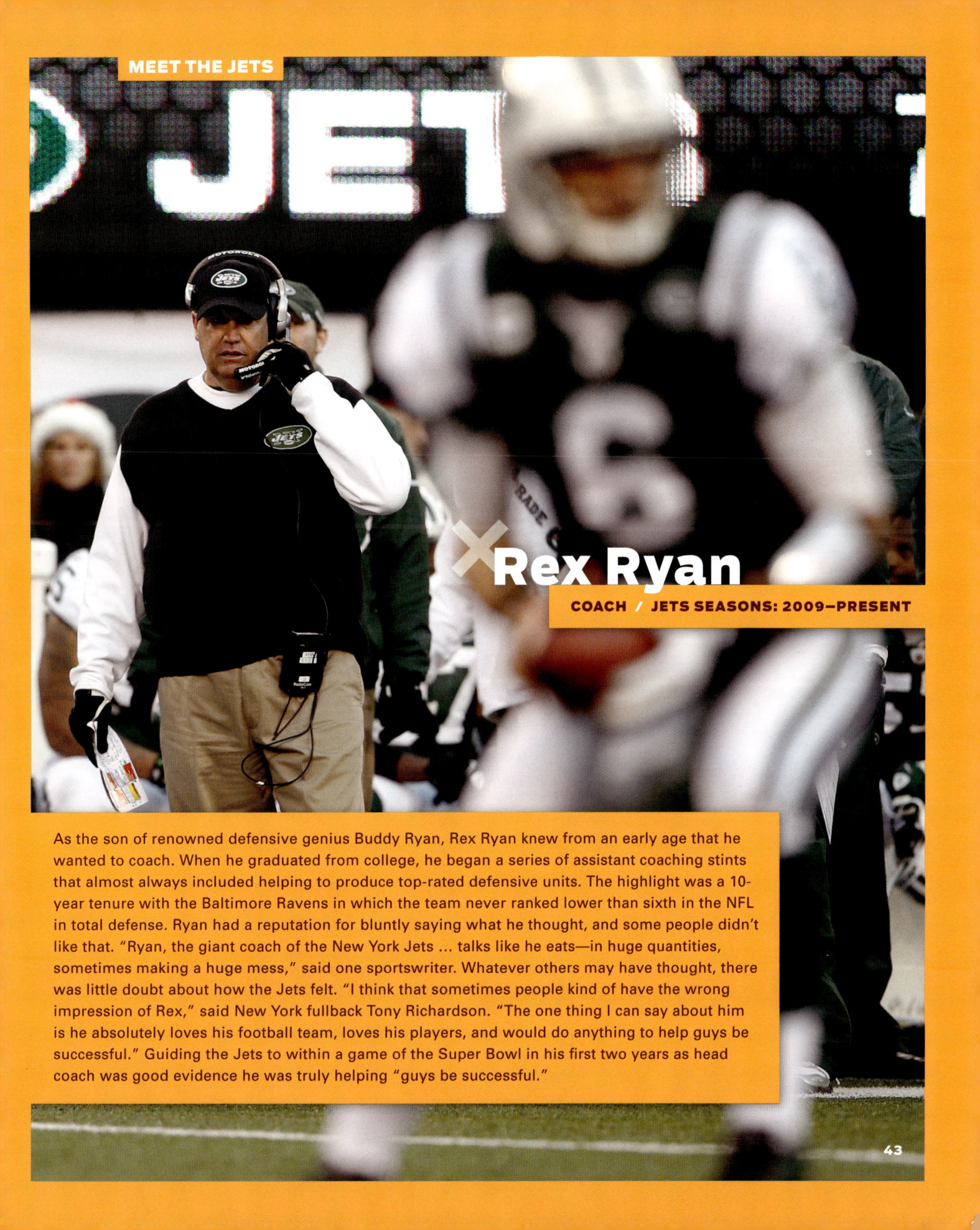

Rex Ryan
COACH / JETS SEASONS: 2009–PRESENT

As the son of renowned defensive genius Buddy Ryan, Rex Ryan knew from an early age that he wanted to coach. When he graduated from college, he began a series of assistant coaching stints that almost always included helping to produce top-rated defensive units. The highlight was a 10-year tenure with the Baltimore Ravens in which the team never ranked lower than sixth in the NFL in total defense. Ryan had a reputation for bluntly saying what he thought, and some people didn't like that. "Ryan, the giant coach of the New York Jets … talks like he eats—in huge quantities, sometimes making a huge mess," said one sportswriter. Whatever others may have thought, there was little doubt about how the Jets felt. "I think that sometimes people kind of have the wrong impression of Rex," said New York fullback Tony Richardson. "The one thing I can say about him is he absolutely loves his football team, loves his players, and would do anything to help guys be successful." Guiding the Jets to within a game of the Super Bowl in his first two years as head coach was good evidence he was truly helping "guys be successful."

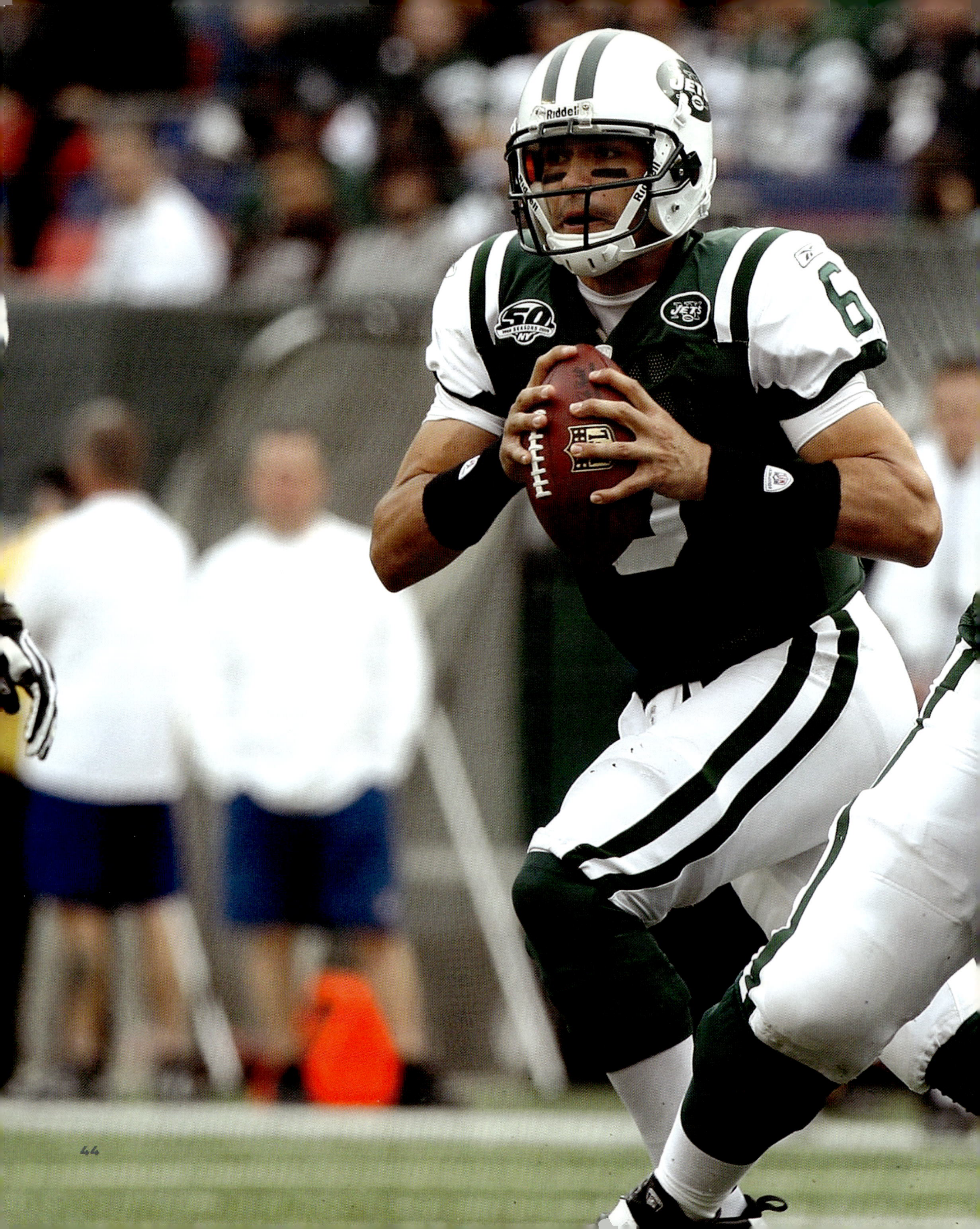

NEW YORKERS AT FIRST HAD HIGH HOPES FOR MARK SANCHEZ

TIM TEBOW STARTED ONLY TWO GAMES IN 2012, STIFLING HIS PASSING ATTEMPTS

DARRELLE REVIS BECAME ONE OF THE NFL'S TOP SHUTDOWN CORNERBACKS

wins and a playoff victory in 2011, inspiring a phenomenon known as "Tebowmania." "I think what we've become is a diverse, more dynamic offense that's going to make it more difficult for opposing teams to defend," said Jets general manager Mark Tannenbaum.

Tannenbaum wasn't much of a prophet. Neither Tebow nor the Jets ever gained any traction in the 2012 season, which ended with a disappointing 6–10 record. Though Sanchez was largely ineffective, Tebow never really had a chance to show what he was capable of doing. Coach Ryan finally benched Sanchez late in the season, replacing him with second-year quarterback Greg McElroy, who had thrown only seven passes and been inactive for all but one game. McElroy was gone after a single start, with Sanchez back under center. Near the end of the season, NFL.com reporter Kimberly Jones commented, "Say this for the Jets: Truly, there's never a dull moment. In a week where the New York Giants no longer control their NFC East destiny and play a must-win game in Baltimore, they have been a sidebar in the metropolitan area. The Jets and their zaniness trump all."

It has been more than four decades since Joe Namath guaranteed—and then delivered—a Super Bowl victory to the Jets faithful. Today's stars in kelly green and white would like nothing more than to collect another Lombardi Trophy—especially since their cross-city rivals, the Giants, have picked up a pair of world championships in the last half decade. When that day comes, there will undoubtedly be one big party in the Big Apple.

INDEX

AFC Championship Game 24, 29, 42
AFL championship 18
AFL Championship Game 10, 17, 18
AFL seasons 8, 11, 12, 13, 15, 16, 17, 18, 21
AFL-NFL merger 16, 21
Anzalone, "Fireman Ed" 41
Atkinson, Al 18
Barkum, Jerome 21
Baugh, Sammy 10
Becht, Anthony 33
Boozer, Emerson 15, 22
Brien, Doug 33
Byrd, Dennis 25
Chrebet, Wayne 28, 29
Coleman, Marcus 32
Coles, Laveranues 39, 40
Cotchery, Jerricho 39
division championships 18, 29, 30
Dorow, Al 11
Edwards, Herm 30, 33, 34
Elliott, Jumbo 32
Ewbank, Weeb 12, 21
Favre, Brett 39
first season 11
Gastineau, Mark 23
Giants Stadium 24, 26
 see also Meadowlands
Greene, Shonn 42
Groh, Al 30, 32
Harper, Bruce 41
"The Heidi Game" 17
Hess, Leon 26, 29
Jets name 12
Johnson, Keyshawn 29
Johnson, Woody 16

Jones, Thomas 40
Klecko, Joe 20, 23, 24
Kotite, Rich 26
Kroll, Alex 13
Lyons, Marty 23
Mangini, Eric 34, 39, 40
Martin, Curtis 29, 33, 34, 38
Mawae, Kevin 29
Maynard, Don 10, 11, 12, 15, 20
McCareins, Justin 33
McElroy, Greg 47
McMillan, Erik 24
McNeil, Freeman 24
Meadowlands 24, 25, 33, 34, 39, 41
Mersereau, Scott 25
Michaels, Walt 21, 23, 24
"Monday Night Miracle" 32
Moss, Santana 33
Namath, Joe 10, 12, 15, 16, 18, 20, 21, 22, 23, 47
"New York Sack Exchange" 23
New York Titans 10, 11, 13
NFL records 10, 15
O'Brien, Ken 24
Parcells, Bill 26, 29, 30, 38
Pennington, Chad 30, 33, 34
Philbin, Gerry 18
playoffs 23, 24, 26, 29, 33, 39, 40, 42
Polo Grounds 11, 13
Powell, Art 11
Pro Bowl 20
Pro Football Hall of Fame 11
retired numbers 20
Revis, Darrelle 40, 42
Richardson, Tony 43

Riggins, John 21
Rookie of the Year award 12
Ryan, Rex 40, 42, 43, 47
Salaam, Abdul 23
Sample, Johnny 18
Sanchez, Mark 40, 42, 47
Sauer, George Jr. 15
Schmitt, John 12, 16
Shea Stadium 12, 16, 18, 23
Shuler, Mickey 24
Slauson, Matt 42
Snell, Matt 12, 15, 21
Super Bowl 16, 17, 18, 21, 22
Tannenbaum, Mark 47
team records 11, 23, 28
Tebow, Tim 47
Testaverde, Vinny 29, 32
Todd, Richard 23
Toon, Al 24
Turner, Jim 17, 18
Walton, Joe 24
Werblin, David "Sonny" 11, 12
Wismer, Harry 8, 10, 11, 13